MOUNTAINS AND CANYONS

FROM THIS EARTH

William Russell

The Rourke Corporation, Inc
Vero Beach, Florida 32964

PHOTO CREDITS
All photos© William Russell except page 13, courtesy of U.S.
Geological Survey

Library of Congress Cataloging-in-Publication Data

Russell, William, 1942–
    Mountains and canyons / by William Russell.
        p. cm. — (From this earth)
    Includes index
    ISBN 0-86593-360-X
    1. Mountains—Juvenile literature. 2. Canyons—Juvenile literature.
[1. Mountains   2. Canyons.]
I. Title II. Series.
GB512.R87 1994
551.4'32—dc20
                                                                94-505
                                                                CIP
Printed in the USA   AC

TABLE OF CONTENTS

MOUNTAINS

Mountains are great mounds and peaks of earth and rock. Mountains stand much taller than the low lands around them.

Some mountains stand apart from other peaks. Other mountains are linked together. These long "chains" of peaks are mountain **ranges**. A mountain range may stretch for thousands of miles.

The height of a mountain is measured upward from sea level. North America's tallest mountain is Mount McKinley at 20,320 feet above sea level.

The Rocky Mountain Range reaches from north to south over thousands of miles of western North America

HOW MOUNTAINS FORM

Scientists believe that most mountains form over millions of years. They begin as sand and mud in the sea. Powerful natural forces—heat and pressure, for example—turn the bits of sand and mud into rock. Movement of the Earth's crust—its outer layer—and other forces deep in the Earth push some of the rocks upward. After millions of years, the lifting resulted in mountains.

Powerful forces deep in the Earth slowly built towers of rock called mountains

KINDS OF MOUNTAINS

Mountains are of many heights and shapes. The newest mountains, scientists say, have the sharpest tops. As mountains age, the wind, rain, and other natural events begin to wear them down. The old, worn tops of the Smoky Mountains in North Carolina and Tennessee are smooth and rounded.

Mountains made by **volcanoes** usually have an upside-down cone shape. These mountains are shaped by fiery, melted rock that gushes upward from a hole in the Earth. The rock spills out into the growing cone shape.

Wind and rain have smoothed tops of New Hampshire's Presidential Range

MOUNTAINS UNDERSEA

If we could drain the oceans, we would see great ranges of mountains that are now undersea. The longest mountain range in the world, the Mid-Atlantic, would be one of them.

The Mid-Atlantic reaches northward 10,000 miles from Antarctica. Iceland is a peak of the Mid-Atlantic Range.

The tallest peaks of the undersea Mid-Atlantic Range form Iceland

*The Grand Canyon of the Colorado River is in
Grand Canyon National Park, Arizona*

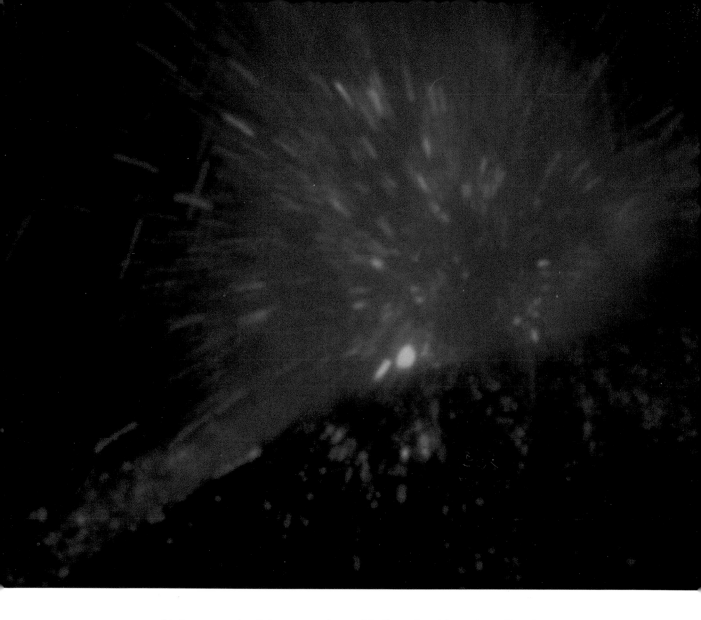

Volcanoes build mountains with fiery liquid rock called lava

WEATHERING

In time, mountains change. The sharp, rough peaks wear away. Mountains become smoother and shorter. This process is called **weathering**.

Most weathering is caused by rain, streams and small particles of sand and rock driven by wind. **Glaciers**, which are great rivers of ice, help wear away some mountains. The action of frost, tree roots and plantlike **lichen** also slowly wears away mountains.

After millions of years, mountains can be reduced to hills.

Weathering slowly reduces a mountain's size

MOUNTAINS ON NATIONAL LANDS

Many of the peaks of North America's greatest mountains are in national parks. These lands are held and protected by the United States and Canada for the enjoyment of everyone.

Jasper, Banff, Kootenay and Waterton Lakes National Parks are in the Rocky Mountains of western Canada. Rocky Mountain, Glacier, Yellowstone, and Grand Teton National Parks are in the Rockies of the United States. Great Smoky Mountains National Park is in the Appalachians.

Mountain peaks in
Jasper National Park, Alberta

CANYONS AND VALLEYS

Valleys are long, low troughs, or ditches, in the Earth. Valleys may be shallow, or "gentle." Valleys with steep walls are known as canyons or gorges.

Most valleys are "dug" by rivers and streams. Moving water tears away rock and soil. Over a long time, the river's bite takes it deeper and deeper into the ground.

A mountain valley in the Alps of Switzerland

CANYONS ON THE NATIONAL LANDS

Some of the spectacular canyons in North America are in national parks. Nahanni National Park in the Northwest Territories of Canada is rugged wilderness. Below the park's peaks, the roaring Nahanni River has cut some of the deepest river canyons on Earth.

Canyonlands National Park in Utah is rich with "red rock" canyons and curious rock forms. The Grand Canyon of the Yellowstone River and its towering waterfalls are highlights of Yellowstone National Park.

The Grand Canyon of the Yellowstone River is in Yellowstone National Park, Wyoming

THE GRAND CANYON

The amazing Grand Canyon of the Colorado River is 277 miles long. In places, it is 18 miles wide and one mile deep! About 3 million people visit this natural wonder each year.

The Colorado River has been carving the Grand Canyon through the rock layers of Arizona for about 6 million years.

In 1869, John Wesley Powell led the first river exploration of the canyon. Powell wisely named it the Grand Canyon.

Glossary

glacier (GLAY shur) — a massive river of ice

lichen (LIE kin) — a plantlike growth that commonly grows on rocks and trees.

range (RANGE) — a long row or "chain" of mountains

volcano (vahl KAY no) — an opening in the Earth and the mountain of rock that forms around it from forces underground

weathering (WEH thur ing) — the wearing away of rock and soil by rain and other weather conditions.

INDEX